REVIVAL OF THE
SECRET PLACE

A Prepatory Guide to a life of Miracles!

REVIVAL OF THE
SECRET PLACE

JEFF JANSEN

Unless otherwise noted, Scripture quotations are from the New American Standard Bible—© Copyright 2002 by The Zondervan Corporation.

Scriptures marked AMP, NIV, NKJV and NLT are from the Amplified Bible, the New International Version, the New King James Version and the New Living Translation, respectively.

To order additional copies of this manual and other valuable resources by Jeff Jansen visit: www.globalfireministries.com.

Cover design: Steve Fryer
Page design: Mark Buschgens – markedbydesign.net

Printed and Manufactured in the United States

ISBN 978-0-9851128-2-0

CONTENTS

LESSON TWO
SOAKING IN THE SECRET PLACE

LESSON THREE
THE BAPTISM OF LOVE AND THE FATHER HEART OF GOD

LESSON ONE

The Holy Spirit of God:
Our Guide into the
Supernatural Kingdom

In this lesson you will learn about the Person of the Holy Spirit—who He is and what He does. We will discuss how He operates in our lives and ministries as well as His relationship to the Kingdom of God. We will also give you a few practical keys that you can use to help you grow in your relationship with the Person of the Holy Spirit.

KEY SCRIPTURE PASSAGES

*For the **kingdom of God is**... righteousness and peace and joy **in the Holy Spirit** (Rom. 14:17).*

*Jesus answered him, I assure you, most solemnly I tell you, that unless a person is **born again (anew, from above)**, he cannot ever **see (know, be acquainted with, and experience)** the kingdom of God.... Unless a man is **born of water and [even] the Spirit, he cannot [ever] enter the kingdom of God**. What is born of [from] flesh is flesh [of the physical is physical]; and what is **born of the Spirit is spirit** (John 3:3, 5-6 AMP).*

*For to us God revealed them through the Spirit; for the Spirit searches all things, **even the depths of God**.... Now we have received, not the spirit of the world, but the Spirit who is from God, so **that we may know the things freely given to us by God,** which things we also speak, not in words taught by human wisdom, but in those **taught by the Spirit...** (1 Cor. 2:10, 12-13).*

And we, who with unveiled faces all reflect the Lord's glory, are being transformed into his likeness with ever-increasing glory, which comes from the Lord, who is the Spirit (2 Cor. 3:18 NIV).

The grace of the Lord Jesus Christ, and the love of God, and the fellowship of the Holy Spirit, be with you all (2 Cor. 13:14).

The Person of the Holy Spirit

The Holy Spirit is a Person we are meant to commune and fellowship with. He is the third Person in the Godhead—completely equal to God the Father and God the Son. The Holy Spirit is God: He is eternal and divine. Some refer to the Spirit of God as an "it" or "itself." Biblically, this is incorrect; the pronouns the Bible always uses to speak of the Holy Spirit are "Him" and "Himself."

In numerous places in Scripture, we see the Holy Spirit portraying characteristics of a Person, comparable to God the Father and God the Son. He demonstrates that He has intellect emotions, thoughts, feelings, and a will. He is omnipresent to believers. He knows the depths of God, making Him all knowing. He is the all-powerful, omnipotent, eternal Spirit of God who has no beginning and no end.

There are many reasons why it is important to understand that the Holy

Spirit is a Person and that He is also God. In the Old Testament, the people of God could say, "We have God *for* us, and we have God *with* us," but they could never say, "We have God in us." New Testament believers are the tabernacles of the Most High God: He lives in us by His precious Holy Spirit becoming one with our spirit. We not only have God *for* us and *with* us, but *in* us and *one spirit* with us!

If the Holy Spirit were simply a power, force, or influence and was not a Person, we would try to do all we could to get a hold of that power. But because the Holy Spirit is a Person, we want Him to get a hold of us. If the Holy Spirit were a force, we would use it to accomplish our will and agenda, and we would eventually slip into pride. But because He is a Person, we partner with Him to accomplish His will; we are humbled by the thought of God wanting to use us. It's not really a matter of attaining something we don't have, rather, it's surrendering to the Holy Spirit so that His power and anointing can flow through us. From a place of humility and brokenness before the Lord, we come to value His all-sufficient grace, which is perfected in our weakness. On many accounts, I've heard that much-repeated Christian phrase, "Faith is spelled R-I-S-K." It's really true. Exercising genuine faith is being positioned in a place of total dependency on our Father in heaven. If you're in a place where you will utterly fail if the Holy Spirit doesn't do something, you're in a really good spot!

The Holy Spirit displays numerous characteristics that only a person could have: He displays intellect by searching and examining the deep things of God; He instructs, teaches, and guides; He has a will, displays emotion, and can speak; He can be insulted, lied to, blasphemed, resisted, and even grieved. ed miracles signs and wonders. This is the season of the love feasts of God.

I. The Holy Spirit is Omnipresent [everywhere–present] to Believers

    A. There is nowhere a believer can go where the Holy Spirit won't be (Ps.139:7-10)

B. When we receive the Holy Spirit, He is with us forever (John 14:16)

C. There is a difference between the *omnipresence* of God and the *manifest presence* of God

    1. The *omnipresence* of God is that all things were created through Christ, so in Him all things hold together and exist (Col. 1:15-17; Eph. 1:23). Also, Christ descended to the depths of hell and has ascended far above all the heavens so He has filled all things (Eph. 4:9-10).

    2. The *manifest presence* of God is when God is tangibly present. Because the Holy Spirit is God, He is the manifest presence of God: God with us. There is nowhere we can go where the manifest presence of God won't be, because we have the Holy Spirit—we have open access to His manifest presence always (John 14:16; Ps. 139:7-10).

II. The Holy Spirit is Omniscient [all knowing]

A. He searches and knows all things, even the depths of God; everything God knows, the Holy Spirit also knows (1 Cor. 2:10)

B. He is intimately acquainted with all of our ways, and the thoughts and intents of our hearts—He knows and sees it all (Ps. 139:1-5; Ps. 94:11; Prov. 15:3)

C. There is no need to instruct the Holy Spirit (Isa. 40:13-14)

D. God will sometimes choose to not remember something or to not see something at all.

    1. God can choose to not remember our sins and transgressions (Isa. 43:25; Heb. 8:12).

2. God chose not to know what was happening in Sodom and Gomorrah for a time, and then He decided to *come down* to see (Gen. 18:20-21).

III. The Holy Spirit is Omnipotent [all powerful]

A. He actively took place in creation: all things originally came into existence through the brooding presence of the Spirit of God (Gen. 1:2).

B. He actively took place in animation: Man became a living soul through the breath of the Spirit (Job 33:4; Gen. 2:7).

C. He actively took place in the resurrection of Jesus, and He brings resurrectionpower and life to our mortal bodies (1 Peter 3:18, NIV; Rom. 8:11).

D. He is eternal – He has no beginning or end (Heb. 9:14)

E. He carries and manifests the power of God (Luke 1:35; Rom. 15:13; Rom. 15:19; 1 Cor. 2:4)

1. Jesus operated in the power of the Holy Spirit with wild demonstrations of miracles, healings, signs, and wonders after He was filled with the Spirit and overcame temptation in the desert (Luke 4:1-15; Acts 10:38).

2. The Holy Spirit gives us power to live victoriously in this life and to preach the Gospel of the Kingdom with demonstrations of power (Acts 1:8; Rom. 15:13; Rom. 15:19; 1 Cor. 2:4; Eph. 3:16; 1 Thess. 1:5; 2 Tim 1:7).

The Holy Spirit in Relationship to the Trinity, and some of His Names

All three persons of the Godhead work, function, and move together in perfect harmony by means of relationship and love. The Trinity is a beautiful example of perfect family relationship, friendship, and intimacy that displays faultless unity in agreement. Jesus came to Earth to glorify the Father. He humbled Himself on Earth when He became a man, and He submitted His life in full obedience to God—even until death (Phil. 2:6-8). Jesus only did what He saw the Father do (John 5:19). The Holy Spirit came from the Father to glorify Jesus Christ. He doesn't speak from His own initiative, but He will disclose to us only what He hears from Jesus (John 16:12-15). Our Father in heaven loves Jesus and has placed all things in His hands and shows Him all things (John 3:35; John 5:20). After the Father redeemed the house of Israel, they decided to rebel against God and grieve His Holy Spirit. God loves His Spirit so much that He actually turned against all of Israel. He became their enemy to fight against them! (Isa. 63:9-10). From meditating on the names of the Holy Spirit that relate to the Father and the Son, we can gain a deeper revelation of the unity and harmony of the Godhead.

The Holy Spirit has many other names that reveal who He is and what He does. His names expose His character and His ability—His heart and His job description. Each name reveals a special and unique facet of who He is and how He operates in the lives of believers.

I. Names of the Holy Spirit that Directly Relate to the Trinity

A. Holy Spirit: Holy [as opposed to unholy], Spirit [as opposed to flesh or the natural, no natural or fleshly body] (Ps. 51:11; Matt. 1:18; Matt. 3:11; Acts 15:28; Rom. 1:4)

B. Spirit of God [Prophecy, Power, Guidance, Dwells in us, etc.] (Gen. 1:2; 1 Sam. 10:10; Ezek. 11:24; Matt. 12:28; Rom. 8:14; 1 Cor. 3:16)

    C. Spirit of the Lord [Victory, Triumph, Power, Freedom, etc.] (Judg. 6:34; Isa. 59:19; Luke 4:18; 2 Cor. 3:17)

    D. My Spirit [Intimate bond in the Trinity] (Gen. 6:3; Joel 2:28; Zech. 4:6)

    E. Spirit of the Living God (1 Cor. 3:3, 6; 2 Cor. 3:1-6)

    F. The Power of the Highest (Luke 1:35)

    G. Spirit of Christ (1 Peter 1:10-11; 2 Peter 1:21)

    H. Spirit of Jesus (Acts 16:17; Phil. 1:19)

    I. Spirit of His Son (Gal. 4:6-7)

II. Other Names of the Holy Spirit

    A. Spirit of Adoption (Rom. 8:14-15, 23)

    B. Spirit of Glory (1 Peter 4:14)

    C. Spirit of Grace (Heb. 10:28-29)

    D. Spirit of Grace and Supplication (Zech. 12:10)

    E. Seven Spirits of God: Spirit of the Lord, Spirit of Wisdom and Revelation, Counsel and Might, Knowledge and the Fear of the Lord (Isa. 11:2)

    F. Spirit of Life (Rom. 8:2)

    G. Holy Spirit of Promise (Eph. 1:13)

    H. Spirit of Truth (John 14:17)

    I. Comforter, Helper (John 14:16)

    J. Eternal Spirit (Heb. 9:14)

    K. The Spirit (John 1:32-33; John 3:5-6)

The Holy Spirit is our Kingdom Guide

Jesus didn't come to Earth so that He could start a religion. He wasn't nailed to the cross so that we could do church. Jesus came to establish and advance the multidimensional, supernatural, heavenly Kingdom on the earth.

What is God's will? His Kingdom. What should Earth look like? Heaven. How do we know this? Because this is how Jesus taught us to pray: *"Your kingdom come. Your will be done, on earth as it is in heaven"* (Matt. 6:10). Jesus modeled flawlessly what it looks like to manifest the Kingdom of heaven on Earth. He demonstrated miracle after miracle, He walked in perfect love, He overcame temptation, He lived righteously, and He revealed the Father. How was He able to do this? Was it because He walked as God on Earth? Nope.

The Bible says that Jesus emptied Himself, took the form of a bondservant, and was made in the likeness of men (Phil. 2:7). Jesus never performed a single miracle on the earth as God. Every supernatural feat He displayed was as a man in right relationship with God. He showed us what *any Spirit-filled man* could *do* and *be* when in right relationship with the Father.

So what was His secret? Why did the power of God flood His ministry? How do we allow the power of God to move through our lives to manifest the Kingdom of heaven on earth? ... It's through intimacy with the Person of the Holy Spirit!

I. The Holy Spirit Manifests the Kingdom:The Kingdom is in the Holy Spirit

    A. *For the* **kingdom of God is**... *righteousness and peace and joy in the Holy Spirit* (Rom. 14:17)

    B. *But if I cast out demons by the* **Spirit of God**, *then the* **kingdom of God** *has come upon you* (Matt. 12:28)

    C. Entering the Kingdom through the Spirit (John 3:3-6)

II. Salvation and Growth in the Kingdom of God by the Holy Spirit

A. Salvation and Sanctification: Born from Above

1. Jesus answered him, I assure you, most solemnly I tell you, that unless a person is born again (anew, from above), he cannot ever see (know, be acquainted with, and experience) the kingdom of God.... Unless a man is born of water and [even] the Spirit, he cannot [ever] enter the kingdom of God. What is born of [from] flesh is flesh [of the physical is physical]; and what is born of the Spirit is spirit (John 3:3, 5-6 AMP).

2. The Holy Spirit draws people to Jesus. He always points to Jesus and testifies of Him (John 15:26).

3. The Holy Spirit positions us in Christ. He baptizes us into His body. In Christ we take part in His death, resurrection, and ascension into heaven.

a) For by one Spirit we were all baptized into one body, whether Jews or Greeks, whether slaves or free, and we were all made to drink of one Spirit (1 Cor. 12:13).

b) Or do you not know that all of us who have been baptized into Christ Jesus have been baptized into His death? Therefore we have been buried with Him through baptism into death, so that as Christ was raised from the dead through the glory of the Father, so we too might walk in newness of life. For if we have become united with Him in the likeness of His death, certainly we shall also be in the likeness of His resurrection... (Rom. 6:3-5).

17

c) But God... made us alive together with Christ (by grace you have been saved), and raised us up with Him and seated us with Him in the heavenly places in Christ Jesus... (Eph. 2:4-6).

4. Sanctification comes by the Holy Spirit.

a) ...to be a minister of Christ Jesus to the Gentiles, ministering as a priest the gospel of God, so that my offering of the Gentiles may become acceptable, sanctified by the Holy Spirit (Rom. 15:16).

b) He saved us, not on the basis of deeds which we have done in righteousness, but according to His mercy, by the washing of regeneration and renewing by the Holy Spirit (Titus 3:5).

c) The Holy Spirit applies and sprinkles the blood of Jesus causing us to be sanctified (1 Peter 1:2).

d) The Holy Spirit convicts the world of sin, righteousness, and judgment (John 8:16-11).

5. The Holy Spirit, Resurrection Power, New Life

a) When we are born of the Spirit, we become new creations in Christ (2 Cor. 5:17).

b) But if the Spirit of Him who raised Jesus from the dead dwells in you, He who raised Christ Jesus from the dead will also give life to your mortal bodies through His Spirit who dwells in you (Rom. 8:11).

B. One with the Spirit

When someone is born of the Spirit, the Spirit of God fills the person and becomes one with his spirit—the seed or sperm of God is planted in his heart. Within the tiny seed is the full nature of God.

1. But the one who joins himself to the Lord is one spirit with Him (1 Cor. 6:17).

2. No one born (begotten) of God [deliberately, knowingly, and habitually] practices sin, for God's nature abides in him [His principle of life, the divine sperm, remains permanently within him]; and he cannot practice sinning because he is born (begotten) of God (1 John 3:9, AMP).

3. You have been regenerated (born again), not from a mortal origin (seed, sperm), but from one that is immortal by the ever living and lasting Word of God (1 Peter 1:23, AMP).

C. Spiritual Family

Someone born of the Spirit is born into a spiritual family and becomes a child in a supernatural kingdom with an inheritance because the Spirit of His Son comes to live in his heart (Gal. 4:6-7).

1. His spiritual senses are turned on, and his spirit man is awakened to experience God's entire Kingdom. As he grows from a child into a mature son, his spiritual senses become exercised and trained to discern (John 3:3-6; Eph. 1:17-19; Heb. 5:14).

2. The seed of God in him grows and expands until he fully resembles Jesus. He is predestined to be conformed into the perfect likeness of Christ, which takes place by beholding the glory of the Lord by the Spirit of God (Rom. 8:29; 2 Cor. 3:16-18).

3. Saints of God have an inheritance in the Kingdom and are heirs with Christ—the Spirit testifies this to our spirit (Matt. 25:34; Eph. 1:11, 14, 18; Col. 1:12, 3:24; Heb. 9:15; Rom. 8:16-17).

4. Mature sons of God are continually led by the Holy Spirit (Rom 8:14).

III. The Holy Spirit is our Travel Guide in the Kingdom of Heaven

A. The Holy Spirit is the Giver of Revelation and is our Teacher in the Kingdom of God

1. He is the Spirit of Revelation (Isa. 11:2; Eph. 1:17).

2. I have many more things to say to you, but you cannot bear them now. But when He, the Spirit of truth comes, He will guide you into all truth; for He will not speak on His own initiative, but whatever He hears, He will speak; and He will disclose to you what is to come. He will glorify Me, for He will take of Mine and will disclose it to you (John 16:12-14).

3. But the Helper, the Holy Spirit, whom the Father will send in My name, He will teach you all things, and bring to your remembrance all that I said to you (John 14:26).

4. There are revelatory gifts and manifestations of the Spirit:

    But the manifestation of the Spirit is given to each one for the profit of all: for to one is given the word of wisdom through the Spirit, to another the word of knowledge through the same Spirit, to another faith by the same Spirit, to another gifts of healings by the same Spirit, to another the working of miracles, to another prophecy, to another discerning of spirits, to another different kinds of tongues, to another the interpretation of tongues. But one and the same Spirit works all these things, distributing to each one individually as He wills (1 Cor. 12:7-11 NKJV).

5. See also: 1 Cor. 9-12; Rev. 2:17 Eph. 1:17-19.

B. The Holy Spirit is our Guide throughout supernatural experiences. He is often the initiator of supernatural encounters and is the door to the supernatural realm. In the Spirit, we can experience trances, visions, dreams, angelic visitations, translations, transportations, bi-locations, etc. We should be led by Him in both the spiritual and natural realm—every area of our lives fully submitted to following Him.

1. If we live by the Spirit, let us also walk by the Spirit (Gal. 5:25).

2. For all who are being led by the Spirit of God, these are sons of God (Rom. 8:14).

3. Jesus, full of the Holy Spirit, returned from the Jordan and was led around by the Spirit in the wilderness for forty days, being tempted by the devil (Luke 4:1-2).

4. When they came up out of the water, the Spirit of the Lord snatched Philip away; and the eunuch no longer saw him, but went on his way rejoicing. But Philip found himself at Azotus, and as he passed through he kept preaching the gospel to all the cities until he came to Caesarea (Acts 8:39-40).

5. I was in the Spirit on the Lord's day, and I heard behind me a loud voice like the sound of a trumpet, saying…. Then I turned to see the voice that was speaking with me. And having turned I saw seven golden lampstands; and in the middle of the lampstands I saw one like a son of man, clothed in a robe reaching to the feet…. When I saw Him, I fell at His feet like a dead man. And He placed His right hand on me, saying… (Rev. 1:10, 12-13, 17).

6. After these things I looked, and behold, a door standing open in heaven, and the first voice which I had heard, like the sound of a trumpet speaking with me, said, "Come up here, and I will show you what must take place after these things." Immediately I was in the Spirit; and behold, a throne was standing in heaven, and One sitting on the throne (Rev. 4:1-2).

7. 'And it shall be in the last days,' God says, 'that I will pour forth of My Spirit on all mankind; and your sons and daughters shall prophesy, and your young men shall see visions, and your old men shall dream dreams (Acts 2:17).

8. And the Spirit lifted me up and brought me in a vision by the Spirit of God to the exiles in Chaldea (Ezek. 11:24).

9. He stretched out the form of a hand and caught me by a lock of my head; and the Spirit lifted me up between earth and heaven and brought me in the visions of God to Jerusalem (Ezek. 8:3).

10. Then the angel carried me away in the Spirit into a desert (Rev. 17:3 NIV).

IV. The Power of the Holy Spirit

A. The *indwelling* Person and presence of the Holy Spirit is there to ignite and strengthen our inner man. He imparts courage, hope, strength, and overcoming power—all the things we need to live victorious lives in Christ. He develops the fruit of the Spirit in our lives, molding and transforming our hearts and character until we resemble the glorious Christ of love.

1. *On the other hand I am filled with power—With the Spirit of the LORD—And with justice and courage* (Mic. 3:8).

2. *…that He would grant you, according to the riches of His glory, to be strengthened with power through His Spirit in the inner man…* (Eph. 3:16).

3. *For God has not given us a spirit of timidity, but of power and love and discipline* (2 Tim. 1:7).

4. *Now may the God of hope fill you with all joy and peace in believing, so that you will abound in hope by the power of the Holy Spirit* (Rom. 15:13).

5. As we intimately fellowship and commune with the Holy Spirit, His fruit is grown and manifested in our lives:

But the fruit of the Spirit is love, joy, peace, patience, kindness, goodness, faithfulness, gentleness, self-control; against such things there is no law (Gal. 5:22).

B. The *resting* presence of the Holy Spirit brings a tangible anointing that covers our lives. Miracles, healings, deliverances, signs, wonders, and salvations are a direct result of the *resting* and *abiding* glory and presence of the Holy Spirit. When we are baptized in the Spirit, we are fully immersed in Him and in the anointing—He comes to rest on us. The key is walking in obedience, which keeps Him resting on us. The longer He abides on us as we walk in obedience, the more our character is refined, which allows us to steward more of the power and anointing of God. Just like Jesus, we will leave the desert under the anointing and in the *power of the Spirit*, able to proclaim that the Spirit of the Lord is resting upon us (Luke 4:14-18). The resting presence of the Holy Spirit forcefully advances the Kingdom of God and destroys the work of Satan and his entire kingdom of darkness.

1. *But if I cast out demons by the Spirit of God, then the kingdom of God has come upon you* (Matt. 12:28).

2. *...but you will receive power when the Holy Spirit has come upon you; and you shall be My witnesses both in Jerusalem, and in Judea and Samaria, and even to the remotest part of the earth* (Acts 1:8).

3. *You know of Jesus of Nazareth, how God anointed Him with the Holy Spirit and with power, and how He went about doing good and healing all who were oppressed by the devil, for God was with Him* (Acts 10:38).

4. *...who was declared the Son of God with power by the resurrection from the dead, according to the Spirit of holiness...* (Rom. 1:4).

5. *...in the power of signs and wonders, in the power of the Spirit; so that from Jerusalem and round about as far as Illyricum I have fully preached the gospel of Christ* (Rom. 15:19).

6. *...and my message and my preaching were not in persuasive words of wisdom, but in demonstration of the Spirit and of power, so that your faith would not rest on the wisdom of men, but on the power of God* (1 Cor. 2:4-5).

7. There are power gifts and manifestations of the Spirit:

    But the manifestation of the Spirit is given to each one for the profit of all: for to one is given the word of wisdom through the Spirit, to another the word of knowledge through the same Spirit, to another **faith** *by the same Spirit, to another* **gifts of healings** *by the same Spirit, to another the* **working of miracles,** *to another prophecy, to another discerning of spirits, to another different kinds of tongues, to another the interpretation of tongues. But one and the same Spirit works all these things, distributing to each one individually as He wills* (1 Cor. 12:7-11 NKJV)

Three Keys for Developing your Relationship with the Holy Spirit

*The grace of the Lord Jesus Christ, and the love of God, and the **fellowship of the Holy Spirit**, be with you all (2 Cor. 13:14).*

This whole thing we call "Christianity" is about intimate relationship with God. It's not a set of rules we are forced to obey but a Person we choose to follow, to love, and to spend our entire lives on. There is nothing in this life (or the next for that matter) that can be compared to the surpassing value of knowing Jesus Christ—everything else is rubbish (Phil. 3:8). The momentary afflictions we experience in this life are minor in comparison to the exquisite glory that will be *"revealed to us and in us and for us and conferred on us"* (Rom. 8:18, AMP)!

First and foremost, we are called to love God with all of our heart, soul, mind, and strength (Mark 12:30). At the end of the day, this is what matters most. Ask yourself, "Am I living for myself or for God? Am I living to please man so that I can gain acceptance and approval, or am I staying true to the word of the Lord over my life?"

Listed below are a few keys to help you get started on developing your relationship with the Holy Spirit. Because I go into greater detail in the following lessons on how to hear the voice of God and unlock the supernatural realm, I'm only giving you a few very practical keys to help you get jumpstarted. These keys are foundational for any Christian's walk with the Holy Spirit.

I.   A Passionate Thirst for His Power, His Presence, and His Touch

The Lord pours out His Spirit on dry and thirsty ground. If you want to experience the power of God and the anointing of the Holy Spirit, passionate desperation is often a prerequisite for receiving a touch from above.

A. *For I will pour out water on the thirsty land and streams on the dry ground; I will pour out My Spirit on your offspring and My blessing on your descendants...* (Isa. 44:3)

B. *Draw near to God and He will draw near to you* (James 4:8)

C. *Ask, and it will be given to you; seek, and you will find; knock, and it will be opened to you. For everyone who asks receives, and he who seeks finds, and to him who knocks it will be opened* (Matt. 7:7-8)

D. *If you then, being evil, know how to give good gifts to you children, how much more will your heavenly Father give the Holy Spirit to those who ask Him* (Luke 11:13)

II. Cultivating a Heart of Faith and Belief

A. *And without faith it is impossible to please Him, for he who comes to God must believe that He is and that He is a rewarder of those who seek Him* (Heb. 11:6).

B. *True faith is a matter of the heart, not of the mind:*

*...for with the **heart** a person **believes**, resulting in righteousness, and with the mouth he confesses, resulting in salvation* (Rom. 10:10).

C. From faith to *faith* to **faith**:

*For in the Gospel a righteousness which God ascribes is revealed, both springing from **faith and leading to faith** [disclosed through the way of **faith that arouses to more faith**]. As it is written, The man who through faith is just and upright shall live and shall live by faith* (Rom. 1:17, AMP).

D. See also: Ps. 37:3; Gal. 3:2; Mark 9:23.

III. Total Surrender

Total surrender is one of the most important steps for catapulting you into deeper realms of the Spirit. Unfortunately, it is one of the places most people get hung up. Living in compromise and following the Holy Spirit half-heartedly is like trying to swim across the Atlantic with a millstone strapped to your neck—it's impossible! You can't go where the Holy Spirit wants to lead you if you're not willing to deny yourself and take up your cross. It's decision-making time. When He says, "Go!" will you go? When He says, "No," will you lay it down? Let me tell you: if you choose to follow the Holy Spirit with all your heart and come to Him with open hands, not holding on to anything in this life, but living in complete and total surrender, you won't be sorry, nor will you regret it. There is a greater glory waiting for those who choose to follow Him—a far greater glory.

A. *Then Jesus said to His disciples, "If anyone wishes to come after Me, he must **deny himself**, and take up his cross and follow Me. For whoever wishes to save his life will lose it; but **whoever loses his life for My sake will find it*** (Matt. 16:24-25)

B. *And we are witnesses of these things; and so is the Holy Spirit, whom God has given to those who **obey** Him* (Acts 5:32)

C. ***Submit** therefore to God. Resist the devil and he will flee from you. Draw near to God and He will draw near to you* (James 4:7-8)

D. See also: Acts 5:32; Ps. 62:5; 1 Peter 1:2

REFLECTION QUESTIONS

1. Who is the Holy Spirit?

   _____

   _____

2. What are a few traits of the Holy Spirit that reveal He is both a Person and God? What are a few scriptures that show us this?

   _____

   _____

3. After reading through this lesson, what are two of the Holy Spirit's names that seem the most significant to you? Why?

   _____

   _____

4. What relationship does the Holy Spirit have with the Kingdom of God?

   _____

   _____

5. Explain the process of being born of the Spirit? What are a few things that happen?

   _____

   _____

6. Why should the Holy Spirit be every believer's Guide in the Kingdom? What could be some possible results if a person doesn't follow the direction of the Spirit of God?

_____

_____

7. What are a few main differences between the *indwelling presence* and the *resting presence* of the Holy Spirit?

_____

_____

8. What are the three keys described in this lesson that could be used to help develop your walk with the Holy Spirit? How do you plan on using these keys to unlock deeper realms of the Spirit in your life?

_____

_____

Questions for Group Discussion

1. Why is it important to understand that the Holy Spirit is a Person and not a force? How could not knowing that the Holy Spirit is a Person affect a Christian's walk with the Lord? What would be a few results?

2. Share a significant occasion when you encountered the Holy Spirit—perhaps the first time. What was it like, and how did it affect you? What was the outcome of that experience?

Life Application

Grab your journal or notebook, and get alone with God. Ask the Father to fill you with the Holy Spirit—then wait and be still. Open yourself up to hear from the Holy Spirit, and position yourself to receive from the Lord in an attitude of humility and hunger. Ask the Holy Spirit to come fellowship and commune with you. Ask Him if there is anything in your life He wants you to let go of, and submit to the Lord. Ask if there is anybody He wants you to forgive. Use this time to get right with God through the shed blood of Jesus Christ and the sanctifying work of the Holy Spirit. If you have any questions, ask Him— these could be questions about your calling, the future, your job, or the Bible. You might be surprised at what He reveals. After your experience with the Holy Spirit, remember to write the details of the encounter in your journal or notebook for later reference.

Prayer

Holy Spirit, I invite You to come into my life and fill my entire being with Your presence. I ask that You would apply the shed blood of Jesus Christ over my life—baptize me into His death and sanctify me from all ungodliness. If there is anyone I need to forgive, show me. If there is anything I must confess and ask forgiveness for, show me. It's my desire to follow You my whole life long. I don't want to hold anything back from You—take all of me! I surrender myself to You. I acknowledge that You are God and Lord of my life. Flood every area of my heart with Your life and light. Let there be no untouched corner, and no dark place in me. Fill me, Holy Spirit, with Your presence, power, and anointing. Raise me to new life in Christ Jesus. Impart to me a supernatural hunger to know you intimately, and to fellowship and commune with You daily. All for the glory of Jesus Christ. In His name, Amen!

REVIVAL OF THE SECRET PLACE

The Holy Spirit of God: Our Guide into the Supernatural Kingdom

LESSON TWO

Soaking in the Secret Place

Jesus told us to go into our prayer closets and to close the door behind us, so we could pray to our Father in secret (Matt. 6:6). This lesson is all about drawing close to the Person of Jesus Christ through a type of listening prayer I like to call *soaking*. Soaking prayer is the door that opens the eternal realm of heaven in our lives and releases the knowledge of the glory of the Lord in the earth.

KEY SCRIPTURE PASSAGES

[For my determined purpose is] that I may know Him [that I may progressively become more deeply and intimately acquainted with Him, perceiving and recognizing and understanding the wonders of His Person more strongly and more clearly].... I press on toward the goal to win the [supreme and heavenly] prize to which God in Christ Jesus is calling us upward (Phil. 3:10, 14, AMP).

He who dwells in the secret place of the Most High shall

remain stable and fixed under the shadow of the Almighty... (Ps. 91:1, AMP).

Be still, and know that I am God (Ps. 46:10, NKJV).

...He will baptize you with the Holy Spirit and fire (Matt. 3:11).

And do not get drunk with wine, for that is dissipation, but be filled with the Spirit... (Eph. 5:18, AMP).

...For the kingdom of God is within you (Luke 17:21, NKJV).

...and raised us up with Him, and seated us with Him in the heavenly places in Christ Jesus... (Eph. 2:6).

*If then you have been raised with Christ [to new life, thus sharing His resurrection from the dead], **aim at and seek** the [rich, eternal treasures] **that are above,** where Christ is, seated at the right hand of God. And **set your minds and keep them set on what is above** (the higher things), not on the things that are on the earth. For [as far as this world is concerned] you have died, and **your [new, real] life is hidden with Christ in God** (Col. 3:1-3, AMP).*

*...let us run with endurance the race that is set before us, **fixing our eyes on Jesus,** the author and perfecter of faith, who for the joy set before Him endured the cross, despising the shame, and has **sat down at the right hand of the throne of God** (Heb. 12:1-2).*

What do you mean, "Soaking"?

Soaking is a form a prayer, but not the type that probably comes to mind. Prayer in the western world often looks like a lot of rambling, a lot of asking

God for something, and a lot of "religious duty." Soaking prayer actually has very little to do with talking to God and more to do with listening to Him. Soaking is *posturing* yourself in a place to *receive* from God after *giving* Him all of yourself. Soaking is *positioning* yourself in a place of *stillness* and *quietness*. It is a place of *meditation* and *contemplation* on the Person of Jesus Christ and the indwelling presence of the Holy Spirit—this is a place of genuine, internal *peace* and *rest*.

The reason we use the word "soaking" when referring to this type of prayer comes from the Greek word "baptizo," which is where we get the English word *baptize from*. John the Baptist said that he baptized in water but that Jesus would baptize us in the Holy Spirit and fire (Matt. 3:11). The Greek word *baptizo* means, "to dip." It contains all of the following meanings: *to dip repeatedly, immersing, fully submerging* (as in a sinking ship), *washing or bathing oneself,* and *overwhelming*.

We want to be soaked, fully submerged, repeatedly dipped, washed, bathed, overwhelmed, and consumed with the presence of the Holy Spirit! Like a dry and brittle sponge needs to be dipped in water, we need to be fully submerged and baptized in the river of God's presence until every fiber of our being is filled to overflowing, so we leak and spill out the glory of God everywhere we go. There are two primary Hebrew words translated into the English word "anoint" in the Old Testament: the first word means, "to rub," and the second word means, "to smear." In both cases, it's talking about *rubbing* or *smearing* oil.

The anointing of God is like oil: it's tangible, transferable, and when not properly contained, it has a tendency to get all over everything! Remember, it's the Person of the Holy Spirit who carries the anointing and power of God. When we spend time with Him in the presence of Jesus Christ, the Anointed One, we can't help but have the anointing of God rubbed and smeared deep into our lives and ministries. It gets all over everything!

Jesus said that we would be baptized in the Holy Spirit (Acts 1:5); we would be soaked and completely submerged in the Holy Spirit. Soaking is actually like pickling. You take a cucumber, soak it in vinegar and spices, and over time it turns into a pickle! We want to go into God's presence as a cucumber and come out like a juicy dill! We need to be pickled in the presence of God. Paul says in Ephesians 5:18 not to "…*get drunk with wine, for that is dissipation, but **be filled** with the Spirit.*" The words, "be filled," in this verse denote multiple and continual infillings of the Holy Spirit. Paul is not saying that being filled with the Holy Spirit is a one-time event. In the Greek, it actually means, "be being filled," or a continual infilling and submerging in the presence of God.

There are many ministers of the gospel who have been released into ministry or have had a major breakthrough in their ministry after a season of soaking and ministering to the Lord in the secret place. This was the case for me.

Several years ago, I entered a season of soaking and pressing hard into the Lord. I would spend hours in the glory of God, and I would be lifted into His presence. Often, while going to bed, I would meditate on the presence of God and I would extend myself into the throne room, ministering to the Lord until I fell asleep. On several occasions, the Lord would enter my room and sit at the end of my bed to spend time with me. Other times the glory of God would come over the top of my head as a lamp or a ball of light. During this season, I received many breakthroughs and encounters in the glory of God, but what was about to happen changed my life and ministry forever. After prayer one night, I remember going to bed early, because at that time I was both working and ministering to make ends meet. With my eyes closed and the lights off in the bedroom, the light from the glory of God was so intense that my whole body shook as waves of God's love rippled over me—it was pure ecstasy! That night I was awakened at 11:22 pm by the blast of a trumpet. Two angels with long silver trumpets were standing at the foot of my bed blowing an alarm in my ears. I felt like John's description on the Island of Patmos when he said that he fell like a dead man (Rev. 1:17). The fear of the Lord filled my body, and I was completely undone in the hands of God. The angel on my left blew a trumpet in my left ear. This is what woke me up. The angel on the right was blowing his trumpet in my right ear. What came out, however, wasn't sound, but a hot wind that entered my body and went down into my chest and spirit man, then exploded in electric power. Immediately, I was pulled out of my body, through the roof, through the atmosphere, and through the stars, and I came to rest in a large room in heaven called the "Room of Intercession." I remember thinking that this must have been a dream. As I looked around, I saw men, women, children, and angels all praying over the nations. I saw regions of the earth flash before me in a moment of time. Everything was so surreal that I could scarcely take in what I was seeing. In the experience, I looked around and saw myself lying on the floor, yet I was standing above myself at the same time. As I was watching myself, praise began to flow from my spirit man. When you encounter the presence of God, what is in your heart begins to rise to the surface. I began to worship Him and say, "Lord, you're so awesome... so beautiful... Jesus, you're so wonderful and incredible...." This praise was coming out of my mouth, but I noticed two voices were coming out of me. There was my voice, and the voice of the Holy Spirit; both voices were harmoniously singing and declaring the goodness of the Lord.

This encounter lasted through the evening and into the morning. As I awoke, my eyes were opened to a whole new dimension in the Spirit. I was prolifically seeing angels, beings, and shafts of light that would move through the house like colorful supernatural pathways reaching from my living room into the heavens. My spirit man had awakened to a brand new place in the glory of God. Rainbows would appear in meetings, and clouds of glory would manifest as I would preach. Miracles would explode in the atmosphere with tangible signs of the glory. Often fireballs or honey wheels would be released in meetings, and the whole house would be whacked under the power of God. We were seeing gold teeth, gold dust, gemstones, and other wonderful signs with many healings and creative miracles. God shifted me, the ministry, and our lives—we've never been the same. I believe God granted this encounter because I hungered and thirsted for Him with my entire being. It wouldn't have happened unless I learned to position myself in a place of stillness, rest, and meditation on the goodness of God. Soaking is a key component to receive breakthrough in your life and ministry. The breakthrough is the result of a heart sold out to Him!

The Upward Call and Tabernacling with God

> [*For my determined purpose is*] *that I may know Him* [*that I may progressively become more deeply and intimately acquainted with Him, perceiving and recognizing and understanding the wonders of His Person more strongly and more clearly*].... *I press on toward the goal to win the* [*supreme and heavenly*] *prize to which God in Christ Jesus is* *calling us upward* (Phil. 3:10, 14, AMP).

The whole purpose of soaking, and the entirety of Christianity for that matter, is to walk in a love relationship with Jesus Christ by getting to know Him, His character, and His nature. Throughout Paul's epistles, we see a golden thread—a unique strand—that tied all of his writings together. This golden thread is the upward call of God in Christ Jesus (Phil. 3:14). In other words, it's being heavenly minded, and setting our minds, hearts, and affections on things above where Christ is seated and where we are seated with Him in the heavenly realm (Eph. 2:6; Col. 3:1-3). The author of Hebrews tells us to boldly come before the throne of grace that exists in Heaven (Heb. 4:16) and to set our gaze firmly on Jesus Christ, the risen and ruling King (Heb. 12:2).

> He [God] also has planted eternity in men's hearts and minds... (Eccl. 3:11, AMP).

Soaking in the Secret Place

Both Isaiah and Ezekiel had incredible throne room encounters (Isa. 6:1-13; Ez. 1:26-28). What they saw was beautiful and amazing, yet their understanding and perception was *in part* because they didn't know Christ. John the Revelator was a man like us—a born again, Spirit-filled believer. Something about heaven and the realm of eternity seized his being. When banished to the Island of Patmos, John was given a great opportunity to get to know the resurrected Christ even more. I can imagine him praying and pressing in and worshiping God *in the Spirit* (Rev. 1:10). Undoubtedly, he had read of Isaiah's and Ezekiel's throne room encounters, and he was longing for his own. The next thing you know, he hears a trumpet and a voice, and he is sucked up into the heavenlies to have one of the most amazing encounters ever recorded! Isaiah and Ezekiel saw dimly the throne and the One who sat upon the throne. John saw the same thing, yet he received a greater unfolding of the revelation of the glory of the Lord. Likewise, when we encounter God on His throne, He can reveal different aspects, characteristics, and revelations of His Person and glory.

Paul had a similar experience: *"Boasting is necessary, though it is not profitable; but I will go on to visions and revelations of the Lord. I know a man in Christ who fourteen years ago—whether in the body I do not know, or out of the body I do not know, God knows—such a man was caught up to the third heaven. And I know how such a man... was caught up into Paradise and heard inexpressible words, which a man is not permitted to speak. On behalf of such a man I will boast; but on my own behalf I will not boast, except in regard to my weaknesses* (2 Cor. 12:1-6). Paul and John were both caught up and saw the throne in paradise in the third heaven. John was able to write down the experience, which became the book of Revelation. Paul, on the other hand, was only permitted to speak of the experience to a degree—seemingly for the purpose of staying humble (vs. 6-10). Paul and John's ministries and callings were different. John was not only permitted to share what he saw, but he was also commanded to write it down. Paul's calling was different: he was heavily involved with the body of Christ, church politics, growth, dos and don'ts, etc. Even though Paul wasn't permitted to publically share his experience, the revelations from his third heaven encounter obviously leaked out through his life and in all of his ministry and writings.

Our aim is to know God as intimately as He can be known. The only thing that will quench the thirst for eternity in our hearts is if we respond to the invitation to go up the mountain of the Lord to meet with Him. We must individually and corporately behold the Lord in all of His glory! When we do this—when we are lifted into His presence—His presence comes down. When we spend time in heaven, heaven comes to earth. When our praises go up, His glory comes down. The more time we spend wrapped in the secret place, the more we will drip heaven's presence everywhere we walk on this earth. We become a conduit—a glory dispenser! When we go up to make our home with Him, He comes down to make His home with us. I want God to make His home with me! I want Him to dwell, settle down, rest, and abide on my life! I want Him to tabernacle with me—I want to be His tabernacle!

> *Jesus answered, If a person [really] loves Me, he will keep My word [obey My teaching]; and My Father will love him, and We will come to him and make Our home (abode, special dwelling place) with him* (John 14:23, AMP).

God has always wanted to make His tabernacle in the earth. This was His original intention in the Garden of Eden, and this will be the grand finale in Revelation 22:3, *"'Behold, the tabernacle of God is among men, and He will dwell among them, and they shall be His people, and God Himself will be among them....'"*

Be Still and Know—Entering into Rest

Psalm 46:10 says, *"Be still, and know that I am God."* The word "still" means *idle, quiet,* and *alone.* In this verse, the word "know" takes several phrases to explain the full meaning: *come to know by experience, perceive, find, see, be made known, become known, be revealed,* and *cause to know.*

The Psalmist David was the master of the *Selah.* That word signifies *rest.* It means *to pause and calmly think and meditate in a place of rest and peace.* I can see David journaling psalm after psalm and worshiping God. Then he takes a *Selah:* he pauses and meditates. When he gets more revelation, he would begin writing again; when finished, he would pause and take another *Selah* until he got more revelation. I think he used it as a means of *divine listening.* In the same way, I came to a level of understanding of the Person of God that brought breakthrough in my ministry—all from practicing *Selah,* or divine listening.

> *For the one who has entered His rest has himself also rested from works, as God did from His. Therefore let us be diligent to enter that rest, so that no one will fall, through following the same example of disobedience.... And to whom did He swear that they would not enter His rest, but to those who were disobedient? So we see that they were not able to enter because of unbelief* (Heb. 4:10-11; 3:18-19).

Partaking of His Divine Nature—Beholding and Becoming

I. Partaking of His Divine Nature

    A. *...by which have been given to us exceedingly great and precious promises, that through these you may be partakers of the divine nature...* (2 Peter 1:4).

B. ...Jesus said to them, "I am the bread of life; he who comes to Me will not hunger, and he who believes in Me will never thirst (John 6:35).

II. Beholding and Becoming—Seeing the Face of God

A. ...but whenever a person turns to the Lord, the veil is taken away. Now the Lord is the Spirit, and where the Spirit of the Lord is, there is liberty. But we all, with unveiled face, beholding as in a mirror the glory of the Lord, are being transformed into the same image from glory to glory, just as from the Lord, the Spirit (2 Cor. 3:16-18).

B. For God Who said, Let light shine out of darkness, has shone in our hearts so as [to beam forth] the Light for the illumination of the knowledge of the majesty and glory of God [as it is manifest in the Person and is revealed] in the face of Jesus Christ (the Messiah) (2 Cor. 4:6, AMP).

The Greatest Commandment and the Result of it!

"Teacher, which is the great commandment in the Law?" And He said to him, " 'You shall love the Lord your God with all your heart, and with all your soul, and with all your mind.' This is the great and foremost commandment. The second is like it, 'You shall love your neighbor as yourself.' On these two commandments depend the whole Law and the Prophets'" (Matt. 22:36-40).

There was a corporate prophetic word released sometime in the 90s that was used to shift the Church back into intimacy with the Lord. The word from the Lord was, "Seek My face, not my hand." Prophetic words are "now" words: they aren't meant to build theology, doctrine, or tradition around. Prophetic words release the heart of God during that season at that specific time. This was a much-needed word during that season because many people were pursuing the hand of God (His works) without seeking His face (intimacy and relationship). That was the word of the Lord *then* but not *now*! And the prophetic word of the Lord *today* will not be the prophetic word of the Lord *tomorrow*! Does that make sense? Many people have taken that word and built theology around it—they say we aren't allowed to seek the hand of God: the miracles, healings, gifts, anointings, etc. This is wrong. The Bible clearly instructs us to pursue His gifts, "... *earnestly desire and cultivate the spiritual endowments (gifts), especially that you may prophesy.... But earnestly desire and zealously cultivate the greatest and best gifts and graces (the higher gifts and the choicest graces)* (1 Cor. 14:1; 12:31, AMP). So—I'm trying to drive this home—we need to seek both the *face* of God and the *hand* of God.

However, the face of God and intimacy with Him should be of the utmost concern and our greatest endeavor. It's perfectly fine to go into an intense season of seeking the gifts and greater anointing and breakthrough so the power of God can flow through you to transform other people's lives. But if you find this is all your heart longs for, and you're not cultivating your relationship with Him other than for this purpose, it's time to confess and repent. That's a dangerous place to be!

> *Many will say to Me on that day, 'Lord, Lord, did we not prophesy in Your name, and in Your name cast out demons, and in Your name perform many miracles?' And then I will declare to them, 'I never knew you; depart from Me, you who practice lawlessness'"* (Matt. 7:21-23).

Many people put so much of a priority on ministering to people that they forget true ministry is *an overflow of your relationship with God.* We have a bunch of dry Christians performing their religious duties, which carries no eternal value or weight because it's not out of intimacy with the Holy Spirit. These people often even have the right intentions of wanting to help people! But Jesus said, "...*apart from Me you can do nothing.*" Jesus is saying that apart from abiding in the Vine we can do nothing that has any *eternal weight* or *value.* It may look good in the moment, but it will be burnt up in fire because it's just wood, hay, and stubble:

> Now *if any man builds on the foundation with gold, silver, precious stones, wood, hay, straw, each man's work will become evident; for the day will show it because it is to be revealed with fire, and the fire itself will test the quality of each man's work* (1 Cor. 3:12-13).

The greatest commandment is to love God with everything in us. The second greatest is to love people as we love ourselves. We need to make sure we get this straight. If serving people and ministering to them is more of a priority than walking in relationship and obedience to God, we're getting the commands confused. We first need to be sold out to God, taking up our cross and following Him, practicing purity of heart, mind, and body, and walking in obedience. When we make His face our goal, we will be so filled and flooded with the life, power, and anointing of God that we can't help but love people to wholeness and see their lives transformed.

When we spend time in the secret place, God rewards us openly (Matt. 6:6, NKJV). Nothing can compare with the benefits, results, and outcome of being intimate with Jesus. We begin to hear and discern His voice clearly; He gives us supernatural wisdom and revelation. We are commissioned into our calling; we receive mantles and increase in anointing. As we behold His image, we take on His character and nature. We really become the body of Christ. We are His hands and feet. We are Jesus in the earth. Like the Lord said in Exodus 7:1 concerning Moses, *we become as God to Pharaoh* (the world).

I. Six Ingredients of the Contemplative State

A. Physical Calm (Heb. 4:9-11; Heb. 3:18-19)

B. Focused Attention (Heb. 12:1-2; John 5:19)

C. Letting Be (Ps. 46:10; Phil. 4:6-7)

D. Receptivity (John 15:4-5)

E. Spontaneous Flow (John 7:38-39)

F. Beholding (2 Cor. 3:18)

II. A Contemplative Prayer Model

A. Reflection

Reflection is letting go of everything but the *here and now*. It's laying aside your past—all of your victories and defeats—and your future—all of your desires and concerns. It's meditating on God in the *here and now*. To reflect means to cast all anxieties on Him, for He cares for us.

Practice the presence of God in the room with you at that moment and the inward presence of the Holy Spirit—Christ in you the hope of glory. The entire Kingdom of heaven resides in your spirit man. It's okay to turn inward to hear the voice of God. You can use your imagination to picture the cloud of God's presence wrapping around you. This isn't new age. God gave the imagination to you, and it is a tool to engage heaven. Jesus taught in parables and engaged people's imaginations in order to lead them into a deeper walk with God.

B. Prayer of Quiet

At the center of our being we are hushed. We have entered into a listening stillness. All the outward and inward distractions have been silenced, and our spirit is completely engaged and alert to hear and experience God. We bask in the warmth of His presence as we focus on Him!

C. Ecstasy

Greek word is *ekstasis*, which is most often translated into the English word, "trance." This state of being is granted by the Lord Himself and cannot be achieved by our own efforts. It is a state of being that is completely unaware of its surroundings, and is completely caught up with the Lord.

D. Becoming Completely Still and Beholding Him in all of His Glory

Coming to a place of total stillness during prayer is a great challenge. If we are going to commune with God, first we must become still. Habakkuk went to his guard post to pray (Hab. 2:1). In the early morning, when it was still dark, Jesus departed to a lonely place to pray (Mark 1:35). After an entire day filled with ministry, Jesus went to a mountain to pray. Stillness is not necessarily the goal. It's a means to go deeper with God. It is the door in which we are able to fellowship and commune with the Lord, spirit to Spirit. Coming to a place of total stillness cannot be hurried, forced, or accomplished because of your ability or self-effort; rather, it must be allowed to happen. At a point in your stillness, God begins to take over, and you sense His active flow within you. At this point spontaneous images begin to flow with a life of their own. He speaks, and you hear. He imparts supernatural strength, wisdom, and endowments in this place of stillness.

III. Dealing with Distractions

A. Outward Distractions

There are many outward distractions that could pull you away from pressing into God. If you're at your house, it could be the phone, neighbors, pets, kids, the chores and cleaning, unwanted guests, email, texting, television, etc. At first, when practicing the presence of God, it may be necessary to eliminate outward distractions as much as possible. It's also helpful to set aside time everyday, normally the same time everyday, to pray, meditate, and practice soaking. This helps develop a pattern and a discipline for feasting on God's presence. Later, after doing this for a while, you will actually learn to carry the same presence of God that you experience during your soaking sessions into the work place, school, grocery store, etc. You become a bearer of His glory and power when you learn to stay in the secret place while doing everyday tasks. This happens through continual worship, prayer, adoration, and beholding Him.

B. Inward Distractions

For most people, inward distractions are a little more difficult to take care of than the outward type. When you're pressing in, and all you can think about is your "To do" list, I've found it helpful to take a minute to write down all the things you need to accomplish. This helps remove it from your mind and subconscious because you can refer back to the list later. If you feel a block because of some type of sin, or you're very sin-conscious, confess it, repent, get rid of it, and keep moving forward. It has been nailed to the cross—if you've confessed and God has forgiven you, you must forgive yourself too. If you find that your mind wanders aimlessly, it's helpful to speak in tongues, sing and worship, focus on Jesus, and/or meditate on the Word until your mind becomes still.

REFLECTION QUESTIONS

1. What is soaking? Describe in your own words.

   _____

   _____

2. In the Hebrew, what are the two meanings for the word *anoint?*

   _____

   _____

3. What is the upward call?

   _____

   _____

4. What does the Bible mean when it talks about God making His tabernacle on the earth?

   _____

   _____

5. What are some ways we enter into the rest of God?

_____

_____

6. What is the greatest commandment? Describe what it looks like to walk out that commandment in your life.

_____

_____

7. What are five ingredients for the contemplative state?

_____

_____

8. What are the points described in the contemplative prayer model in this lesson?

_____

_____

Activity and Questions for Group Discussion

1. In a group setting, put on some light worship or instrumental music. Find a comfortable place to sit or lie down. Spend a set amount of time soaking (10 to 30 minutes). Invite the Holy Spirit to come and meditate on His indwelling presence.

2. Get back together and take turns discussing what happened. Did you see or hear anything? Did you feel or sense the presence of the Lord? What were some hindrances or distractions to pressing in? What did the Lord do? Have fun with the discussion and learn from each other's encounters.

Line Application

Grab your journal or notebook, and get alone with God. Quiet yourself, and still your mind before the Lord (Ps. 46:10). If you haven't had much experience doing this, it will take some practice at first. That's right! It actually takes practice and spiritual exercise to learn how to discern the voice of the Holy Spirit. Turning off all the mental noises, thoughts, and concerns is easier said than done. However, you're not necessarily trying to turn them off and become void as many New Agers teach when giving instruction on meditation. We don't want to be void of anything—we want to be filled with Jesus so that He takes over our thoughts, imaginations, desires, etc. As believers, we don't make nothingness the focus of our meditation; *He* is our focus. Oftentimes, when engaging the presence of the Lord, we actually have to sink into ourselves. We're not trying to hear a voice that thunders from heaven—an impersonal force that exists somewhere in the expanse. We are listening for the still small voice that whispers from within. All the treasures of wisdom and knowledge are hidden in the Person of Jesus Christ (Col. 2:3); this same Jesus lives in your heart (Eph. 3:17) and your spirit has been made one spirit with the Holy Spirit (1 Cor. 6:17). Open yourself to hear from the Holy Spirit, and be led by Him. Journal anything you receive or any experience that takes place.

Prayer

Holy Spirit, I position myself before You. I ask You to speak to me and lead me in whatever spiritual experience You choose. Help quiet the thoughts and concerns of the day, and allow my heart and spirit to be fully fixated on You and Your indwelling presence. I'm hungry to see and hear, to feel, and to taste and smell in the spirit realm. I open myself to You and enter the supernatural realm of heaven through the Door—Jesus Christ. I bless You and give You glory. In Christ's name, Amen.

Soaking in the Secret Place

REVIVAL OF THE SECRET PLACE

LESSON THREE

The Baptism of Love and the Father Heart of God

"I AM" is so big and multifaceted that He reveals Himself to mankind throughout the Bible in thousands of different ways. He expresses His character and nature to mankind through His words, His actions, and hundreds of Names. I believe one of the greatest revelations that a person can receive is of *God as their Father*. This lesson on the Father heart of God, and the baptism of love is one of the simplest teachings in this curriculum—yet it is one of the most profound and life-changing if you really get it!

Opening Prayer

Abba Father, I ask that throughout this lesson you would reveal Your nature and character to me more and more. Break off any false mindsets or perceptions that I have of You. I ask you to fill me with the Spirit of adoption until I can approach you with confidence, and I believe that you are for me and not against me. Perfect love casts out all fear. I don't want to have an ungodly fear that You are going to punish or torment me, or that You're always out to get me. Baptize me in your love, and reveal your Father's heart to me. Teach me about my identity as a son of a loving and powerful Father who protects, guides, comforts, and provides for me. Thank you for being a good Dad. In Jesus' name, amen.

KEY SCRIPTURE PASSAGES

So he got up and came to his father. But while he was still a long way off, his father saw him and felt compassion for him, and ran and embraced him and kissed him. And the son said to him, "Father, I have sinned against heaven and in you sight; I am no longer worthy to be called your son." But the father said to his slaves, "Quickly bring out the best robe and put it on him, and put a ring on his hand and sandals on his feet; and bring the fattened calf, kill it, and let us eat and celebrate; for this son of mine was dead and has come to life again; he was lost and has been found." And they began to celebrate (Luke 15:20-24).

Now when all the people were baptized, Jesus was also baptized, and while He was praying, heaven was opened, and the Holy Spirit descended upon Him in bodily form like a dove, and a voice came out of heaven, "You are My beloved Son, in You I am well-pleased" (Luke 3:21-22).

He said to them, But who do you [yourselves] say that I am? Simon Peter replied, You are the Christ, the Son of the living God. Then Jesus answered him, Blessed (happy fortunate, and to be envied) are you, Simon Bar-Jonah. For flesh and blood [men] have not revealed this to you, but My Father Who is in heaven. And I tell you, you are Peter [Greek, Petros—a large piece of rock], and on this Rock [Greek, Petra—a huge rock like Gilbraltar] I will build My church, and the gates of Hades (the powers of the infernal region) shall not overpower

The Baptism of Love and the Father Heart of God

it... (Matt. 16:15-18, AMP, emphasis added).

For all who are being led by the Spirit of God, these are the sons of God. For you have not received a spirit of slavery leading to fear again, but you have received a spirit of adoption as sons by which we cry out, "Abba! Father!" The Spirit Himself testifies with our spirit that we are children of God, and if children, heirs also, heirs of God and fellow heirs with Christ, if indeed we suffer with Him so that we may also be glorified with Him (Rom. 8:14-17).

I will not leave you as orphans... (John 14:18).

[Now] He is the exact likeness of the unseen God [the visible representation of the invisible]... (Col. 1:15, AMP).

And He is the radiance of His glory and the exact representation of His nature... (Heb. 1:3).

There is no fear in love [dread does not exist], but full-grown (complete, perfect) love turns fear out of doors and expels every trace of terror! For fear brings with it the thought of punishment, and [so] he who is afraid has not reached the full maturity of love [is not yet grown into love's complete perfection] (1 John 4:18, AMP).

Yet amid all these things we are more than conquerors and gain a surpassing victory through Him Who loved us. For I am persuaded beyond doubt (am sure) that neither death nor life, nor angels nor principalities, nor things impending and threatening nor things to come, nor powers, nor height nor depth, nor anything else in all creation will be able to separate us from the love of God which is in Christ Jesus our Lord (Rom. 8:37-39, AMP).

But God demonstrates His own love toward us, in that while we were yet sinners, Christ died for us (Rom. 5:8).

The Father Heart of God

As we talked about in the previous lesson, *Soaking in the Secret Place*, genuine Christianity is all about walking with God in intimacy. Our aim and desire is to get to know God as much as He can be known. Paul said, "*[For my determined purpose is] that I may know Him [that I may progressively become more deeply and intimately acquainted with Him, perceiving and recognizing and understanding the wonders of His Person more strongly and more clearly].... I press on toward the goal to win the [supreme and heavenly] prize to which God in Christ Jesus is calling us upward*" (Phil. 3:10, 14, AMP).

One of the greatest revelations we can have is that of the Father Heart of God. Our Father in heaven is faithful, affectionate, generous, and strong, yet He is gentle, attentive, and accepting. He loves you as His beloved child. There is nothing you can *do* or *not do* that will make God love you any more or any less. His love is eternal, uncreated, and perfect.

1 Corinthians 13:4-8 reveals what true love looks like. Because God is love (1 John 4:8, 16), I like to substitute the word, "God," for the word, "Love," using the Amplified Version:

> *God endures long and is patient and kind; God is never envious nor boils over with jealousy, is not boastful or vainglorious, does not display Himself haughtily. God is not conceited (arrogant and inflated with pride); God is not rude (unmannerly) and does not insist on His own rights or His own way, for He is not self-seeking; He is not touchy or fretful or resentful; He takes no account of the evil done to*

The Baptism of Love and the Father Heart of God

Him [pays no attention to a suffered wrong]. He does not rejoice at injustice and unrighteousness, but rejoices when right and truth prevail. God bears up under anything and everything that comes, God is ever ready to believe the best of every person, His hopes are fadeless under all circumstances, and He endures everything [without weakening]. God never fails [never fades out or becomes obsolete or comes to an end] (1 Cor. 13:4-8, AMP).

This kind of love puts things in perspective, huh? Does this conflict with some of your perceptions of God? If God doesn't express *all* of the characteristics above, how then are we expected to express them? In the core of God exists all of the expressions listed above, and it's the nature of God's love perfected in us that is released through us: "*We have come to know and have believed the love which God has for us. God is love, and the one who abides in love abides in God, and God abides in him. By this, love is perfected with us, so that we may have confidence in the day of judgment; because as He is, so also are we in this world*" (1 John 4:16-17).

Many people have perceptions of God the Father and God the Son that are completely contrary. They see Jesus as their Savior, Lord, Friend, Lover, big Brother, accepting, forgiving, generous, and an all-around nice guy. But then they think of God the Father: He might express a *few* of the same characteristics Jesus displayed, but He's still a little rough around the edges, a little distant, a little cold-hearted, and a little too busy to hang out. Why is this? God obviously isn't bipolar!

One of the primary reasons most people have a hard time connecting with God the Father is because they have had false perceptions imbedded in their minds and hearts since childhood. Oftentimes, people view God as they see their own Father or some other type of authority figure. If your earthy father was always too busy for you, you might feel as if your heavenly Father is distant also. If your earthly father was only pleased with you when you behaved right, and often disciplined you out of anger, you'll likely feel that your heavenly Father doesn't love you if you make a mistake, and that He is cold-hearted, unforgiving, impatient, and simply angry. You'll feel the need to do things perfectly to earn God's love. If your motivation for walking in righteousness, loving and ministering to people, and being a "good" Christian is to gain God's acceptance or approval, you need a deeper revelation of the love and grace of the Father heart of God. Things that your parents said during your childhood planted seeds in your heart that molded you as you grew. If your dad said, "Don't cry! Real men don't cry…" you'll probably grow up holding back your emotions and have a hard time expressing who you really are—even around God! If he said, "Don't speak unless spoken to…" you'll probably grow up feeling insignificant, and that you have nothing important to say. How many prophetic voices do you think have been quenched because people don't believe they carry the word of the Lord? When mom or dad said not to speak unless spoken to, the enemy came and robbed that child's voice—he robbed the word of the Lord!

I'm sure we can all look back and see where our parents messed up a time or two, or maybe they were just blatantly evil people. Holding these things against them won't help. If the Holy Spirit brings something like this to light, thank Him for showing you, forgive your parents, and allow the Holy Spirit to touch the deep places of your being.

God is a family man—what was He thinking when He made families? Psalm 68:6 says, "*God makes a home for the lonely…*." God creates families to express His love and nature. He wants parents to raise their children as He would raise them and to set an example of living in love: "*Fathers, do not irritate and provoke your children to anger [do not exasperate them to resentment], but rear them [tenderly] in the training and discipline and the counsel and admonition of the Lord* (Eph. 6:4, AMP). But as we've discussed, there's no such thing as a perfect family or a perfect parent. We are called to follow God's example because He is the perfect Father (Matt. 5:48). As we get close to God, false mindsets about Him are stripped away. In the light of His glory, He is revealed to us in indescribable ways that shatter old paradigms that we embraced about Him. The more we see Him, the more we are made like Him (1 John 3:2-3; 2 Cor. 3:18). The more we get to know our Father in heaven, the more we have the ability to imitate Him and grow into His image: *"Therefore be imitators of God, as beloved children; and walk in love..."* (Eph. 5:1-2).

When our perceptions of the Father and Jesus contradict each other, we need to allow the Holy Spirit to reprogram our minds and hearts. Anytime we have a question about the nature of God, all we have to do is look at Jesus Christ.

> *[Now] He [Jesus Christ] is the exact likeness of the unseen God [the visible representation of the invisible]...* (Col. 1:15, AMP, emphasis added).

> *And He [Jesus Christ] is the radiance of His glory and the exact representation of His [God's] nature...* (Heb. 1:3, emphasis added).

God revealing Himself in the Old Testament was only a partial revelation. In order to see the full expression and image of God, we simply have to look at Christ. He is the image of the invisible God, the exact representation of God's nature.

Group Activity

Get in a group of two to five people with Bibles in hand, and look over the six aspects about God listed below. Discuss false views that people might have about God the Father. Discuss some of the views you hold about God's character and nature. Then, with a concordance, a computer Bible study program, or an online website such as www.biblegateway. com, find out what the Bible has to say about each point below. Cite

Scripture verses that plainly tell us about the nature of God; also, cite Scripture verses that show us God's nature by something He said or did. Remember, the points below are expressions of God's nature towards His children and His followers. Using Old Testament passages concerning Israel and the enemies of God could be a partial revelation of the nature of God and not the full expression found in Jesus Christ. However, there are numerous Old Testament verses that give us a glimpse of the greater unfolding revelation of the love and goodness of God revealed in the New Testament. Since Jesus is the expression of the Father you can apply any passage you find about Him to the nature of Father God.

Remember, the parables Jesus taught in the Gospels are good places to learn about the nature of God. Here are a few Scripture passages that will help jumpstart those mental muscles and Bible study skills: 1 John 4:18; Hebrews 12:4-11; Jeremiah 33:6-9; Jeremiah 29:11-14; Exodus 33:18-19; 2 Timothy 2:13; 1 Corinthians 1:9; James 1:5; Hebrews 13:5-6; Psalm 37:3-5; Hosea 11:4; 1 Peter 5:7; Zephaniah 3:17; Psalm 139:1-18; Romans 15:7; Luke 15:11-32; Romans 8:15; Ephesians 1:6, NKJV; Philippians 4:19, AMP.

- Our Father's Discipline and Authority

_____

_____

- Our Father's Faithfulness

_____

_____

The Baptism of Love and the Father Heart of God

- Our Father's Generosity

_____

_____

- Our Father's Affection

_____

_____

- Our Father's Attentiveness

_____

_____

- Our Father's Acceptance

_____

_____

Life Application

After completing the above activity with a group, grab your journal, and get alone with God. Allow those verses to sink into your spirit. Spend some time worshiping and speaking in tongues. Ask the Father what He thinks about you. Then, open yourself to allow the Holy Spirit to write through you. With your pen and journal, ask the Lord to write His thoughts towards you. Begin to journal what you would imagine Father God saying about you if He wrote you a love letter. Ask Him what He likes about you. Ask Him why He loves you. Ask Him to share some of His thoughts. Don't think too much... just let the Spirit of God bubble up in you. I believe much of the Bible was written when the authors postured themselves to hear God like this.

The Baptism of Love—Intimacy Releases Identity

*Now when all the people were baptized, Jesus was also baptized, and while He was praying, heaven was opened, and the **Holy Spirit descended upon Him** in bodily form like a dove, and a voice came out of heaven, "You are My beloved Son, in You I am well-pleased"* (Luke 3:21-22).

I love this verse! When you are baptized in the Holy Spirit, you are baptized with the Spirit of adoption: *"For [the Spirit which] you have now received [is] not a spirit of slavery to put you once more in bondage to fear, but you have received the Spirit of adoption [the Spirit producing sonship] in [the bliss of] which we cry, Abba (Father)! Father"* (Rom. 8:15, AMP). We are accepted into the family of God. No longer is God a distant force in a heavenly realm some place far away; He becomes our Dad, our Abba, our Papa, and our Father. He's someone who we can approach with confidence, knowing that He loves us. We don't have to hide from Him because of sin—that was taken care of on the cross. We don't have to fear Him because we think He's against us, or waiting to catch us doing something bad so that He can punish us. We no longer need to have an unhealthy type of fear that thinks we are going to be tormented (1 John 4:18). God is for us, not against us (Rom. 8:31).

Many people look at the above verse and see clearly that Jesus was baptized in the Holy Spirit. Afterwards, He was led into the desert so that He could overcome the devil. What people fail to realize is that God says, *"You are My beloved Son, in You I am well-pleased."* I like to call this the Baptism of Love.

Take note: Jesus hadn't started His ministry yet. He hadn't cast out a demon, performed a miracle, healed a sick person, or preached a single message. Why did God say that He loved Him and that He was pleased with Him? It's simply the nature of God and the extravagance of His unconditional, uncreated, multifaceted love. God loved Jesus not because of all the awesome stuff Jesus did, but because He loved Him and was pleased in Him; Jesus was His Son. God loves His children!

Jesus was not only baptized in the Holy Spirit, but He was also baptized in the Father's love. This gave Him strength to conquer the enemy and to make it through the next 40 days in the desert.

What do you find your identity in? If someone was to ask you, "Who are you?" what would you say? Someone might respond with their job title: "I'm a dentist"; or someone might reply with their calling and function in the Kingdom: "I'm an evangelist." That really doesn't answer the question. That's not *who* you are. You don't find your identity in what you *do*; you find it in relationship with God. You are His child—His son or daughter. Some people find their identity in their possessions—in what they own. You can't find your identity in your belongings; you find it in who you *belong to*. Identity is knowing *who* you are and *whose* you are.

So who are you? The answer to the question is "I'm a son of God." Identity as a son or a daughter of God is birthed out of intimacy and relationship with Him. *Intimacy* releases *identity* and *identity* releases *destiny*. Walking in relationship with Father God breaks off all fear and worry. How many people are plagued with worry? We tend to worry about money, food, relationships, clothes, jobs, etc. Anything that can be worried about, we tend to worry about it. Knowing that God is your Father breaks off all that worry (Matt. 6:25-34) and helps propel you into your destiny.

Identity Theft—Identity Releases Destiny

When Jesus was baptized in the Holy Spirit and in the Father's love, there was a supernatural strength imparted into Him so He could overcome everything satan threw at Him over the next 40 days in the desert.

> *Jesus, **full of the Holy Spirit**, returned from the Jordan and was led around by the Spirit in the wilderness for forty days, being tempted by the devil. And He ate nothing during those days...* (Luke 4:1-2).

As recorded in the Bible, Satan came to Jesus three times and tried to get Him to deviate from His calling to establish the Kingdom of God in the earth. We can learn several things from Jesus' 40-day desert experience, but one thing I would like to point out is that two out of the three times Satan tempts Jesus, he says, *"If You are the Son of God...?"* What was Satan questioning? He was questioning Jesus' identity as God's Son. One minute, Jesus is baptized in the Father's love and a loud voice from heaven says, *"You are My beloved Son, in You I'm well-pleased"* (Luke 3:22); the next minute, Satan says, *"If You are the Son of God..."* (Luke 4:3, 9). Satan was trying to get Jesus to second-guess His identity as the Son of God, ultimately robbing Him of His calling and destiny in the earth. Let's take a look at this account:

> *And the devil said to Him, **"If You are the Son of God,** tell this stone to become bread." And Jesus answered him, "It is written, 'Man shall not live on bread alone.'" And he led Him up and showed Him all the kingdoms of the world in a moment of time. And the devil said to Him, "I will give You all this domain and its glory; for it has been handed over to me, and I give it to whomever I wish. Therefore if You worship before me, it shall all be Yours." Jesus answered him, "It is written, 'You shall worship the Lord Your God and serve Him only.'" And he led Him to Jerusalem and had Him stand on the pinnacle of the temple, and said to Him, **"If You are the Son of God,** throw Yourself down from here; for it is written, 'He will command His angels concerning you to guard you,' and, 'on their hands they will bear you up,*

so that you will not strike your foot against a stone.'" And Jesus answered and said to him, "It is said, 'You shall not put the Lord Your God to the test.'" When the devil had finished every temptation, he left Him until an opportune time (Luke 4:3-13).

So much of what we wrestle with in our lives is over identity. Television advertisements try to make you feel like you *absolutely need* to buy their product. One of the tactics is to attack your sense of identity. In order for you to be truly *happy* and *fulfilled*, and in order for you to be *cool* and *accepted*, you need to buy this product! The reality is that genuine fulfillment comes from the Father's love, not by worrying about your reputation or what people think.

When you sin, does the enemy come and say to you, "See, you sinner! You messed up again... God isn't going to accept you!"? Or what about, "You're not even born-again" or "You're worthless...."? These are all lies of the enemy that get you to question your identity as a child of God and your value and worth to Him. This is why Satan is called the accuser of the brethren (Rev. 12:10): he is always pointing his finger! When God speaks to us, it's never a voice of accusation—He doesn't make us feel guilty or condemned (Rom. 8:1). The Holy Spirit does, however, *convict* us of sin (John 16:7-8), but when He speaks it always imparts love, mercy, grace, and strength into our inner man (Eph. 3:16), so we can overcome whatever we're wrestling with. His word lifts us from the pit.

Jesus entered the desert *full* of the Holy Spirit, and after 40 days, He left the desert in the *power* of the Holy Spirit (Luke 4:1, 14). There was a strengthening that happened in His identity as a Son of God when He was tempted and overcame Satan. Every time we go through a trial season and we overcome, something is solidified inside of us. We're not only *filled* with the Holy Spirit, but we also begin to operate in the *power* of the Holy Spirit. If we're in a season of difficulty, oftentimes a season of promotion is right around the corner. Jesus left the desert in the power of the Spirit, completely ready to start His ministry.

*And Jesus returned to Galilee in the **power of the Spirit,** and news about Him spread through all the surrounding district. **He began teaching in their synagogues**.... And the book of the prophet Isaiah was handed to Him, And He opened the book and found the place where it was written, "The Spirit of the Lord is upon Me, because He anointed me to preach the gospel to the poor. He has sent me to proclaim release to the captives, and recovery of sight to the blind, to set free those who are oppressed, to proclaim the favorable year of the Lord." And He began to say to them, "**Today this Scripture has been fulfilled in your hearing**"*
(Luke 4:14-15, 17-19, 21).

"Today this Scripture has been fulfilled in your hearing..." Jesus had a destiny and a calling in the earth; He had a mission. He was commissioned into His *destiny* after solidifying His *identity*, which was birthed from *intimacy* with the Father and understanding the Father heart of God.

But who can endure the day of His coming? And who can stand when He appears? For He is like a refiner's fire and like fullers' soap. He will sit as a smelter and purifier of silver, and He will purify the sons of Levi and refine them like gold and silver, so that they may present to the LORD offerings in righteousness (Mal. 3:2-3).

We must draw close to the heart of God and allow Him to mold and shape our character. We must receive the baptism in the Father's love and let His Word wash over us. We must embrace the presence of God and lean on Him completely in those seasons of purification and purging. Why? Because when it's all through, we come out in the *power* of the Spirit, as gold refined by fire—commissioned into our Kingdom destinies that will turn the world upside down!

REFLECTION QUESTIONS

1. Why is getting a revelation of the Father heart of God so important?

_____

_____

2. What does it mean to you that God is your Father?

_____

_____

3. What does it mean to you that you are a child of God?

_____

_____

4. What are some false mindsets that you've had about Father God in the past?

_____

_____

5. What are some things that your earthly father—or an authority figure—did or didn't do that gave you a false perception of the character of God?

_____

_____

6. In what do you find your identity? Explain what that means.

_____

_____

7. What gives birth to genuine identity and destiny? Explain.

_____

_____

8. Describe a desert season you went through, where you learned something about the nature of God and/or yourself. Explain what you learned.

_____

_____

Questions for Group Discussion

1. What is the Father heart of God? Why is it so important to know the Father's heart? Explain the baptism of love. Do you think this is a one-time event, or does it happen multiple times? How do we get to know the heart of God more?

2. What are some ways the enemy has tried to pull you from your identity as a child of God? What happened?

Prayer

Father God, thank you for Your goodness, Your faithfulness, Your mercy, and Your unfathomable, uncreated, unconditional love. I love You. Reveal more of Yourself to me. I open myself to You to teach me more and more about Your character and nature. Help reprogram those false perceptions and mindsets I've embraced of You. Help me not place my identity in what I do or in what I own. Teach me about my identity as a Son of God. In Jesus' name, Amen!

The Baptism of Love and the Father Heart of God

REVIVAL OF THE SECRET PLACE

Global Fire Creations

visit our website at: www.globalfirecreations.com

RECEIVE A FREE GIFT

Subscribe to our e-newsletter and receive a
free downloadable gift

visit: www.globalfireministries.com to subscribe

To Purchase Additional

Global Fire Creations

Products visit: www.globalfirestore.com

KINGDOM LIFE INSTITUTE

- Get saturated in the Presence & Word of God for 9 months.
- Learn how to study the Bible on a whole new level.
- Receive impartation & training from some of today's leading generals in the Body of Christ.
- Mature in the Prophetic, Healing, and Miracle ministries.
- Connect with a Kingdom family and make friends for life.
- Three-year program available for those who want more!

GET STARTED TODAY!
Scholarships and Payment Plans Available

Founded by:

Jeff Jansen and Eric Green

Endorsed By:

Bob Jones, Larry Randolph, David Hogan, Mahesh Chavda, James Goll,
Patricia King, Ray Hughes, Bobby Conner, James Maloney, Jake Hamilton

www.kingdomlifeinstitute.com

ALSO AVAILABLE
From the Global Fire Store

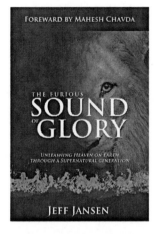

Glory Rising:
Walking in the Realm of Creative
Miracles, Signs and Wonders

The Furious Sound of Glory:
Unleashing Heaven on Earth
Through a Supernatural Generation

**In Search of the
Face of God**
2 CD Teaching Series

The Sound of Glory:
Soaking CD by Jeff Jansen and
Julian & Melissa Wiggins

These and many more faith-building and
encouraging products are available from
www.globalfirestore.com

Other Books by Jeff Jansen

Cum Christo Enthroned

*The Believers' Guide to
Miracles, Healing, Impartation
& Activation*

*The Furious Sound of Glory:
Unleashing Heaven on Earth
Through A Supernatural Generation*

*Glory Rising: Walking in the Realm
of Creative Miracles, Signs & Wonders*

*Glory Rising Manual: Keys to
Understanding the Glory*

Adventures in the Prophetic